The Goal Getter Guide
A simple strategy to make your goals your reality

The Goal Getter Guide
Copyright © 2017 Clarity Cove Publishing/ CreateSpace Publishing

All Rights Reserved. No part of this book can be scanned, distributed or copied without permission.

Cover Art by Perfect Designs

Foreword by Nik Carson

Interior Design by Nicolya Williams

For more information email Nicolya@nicolyawilliams.com

For every woman who feel that reaching goals is impossible. I am here to show you that your biggest dreams can come true!

Dedication

This book is dedicated to my two daughters Kaelyn and Kamryn.
They are the very reason I dream BIG!

Acknowledgments

The first acknowledgement goes to my Heavenly Father and Jesus Christ. This book would not be possible without you. I honor you and praise you for all that you have done in my life and all that you continue to do. I love you!

To my daughters, Kaelyn and Kamryn, you two are my biggest blessings. I tell you both all the time that you motivate me but I can't stress that enough. I set out to write this book in the midst of the hardest time in my life but I set a goal. I wanted to be an example to you both that despite what is going on in the physical realm God is in control and that we can push through and do anything that we set our minds to. I hope that you always continue to dream big. No matter what, mommy loves you and there is NOTHING you can do about it!

To my spiritual mentor Alina, I am so grateful that you were strategically placed in my life at just the right moment. I thank God for you because you have been such a blessing to me and for that I am extremely grateful. I love you.

Welcome to *The Goal Getter Guide.* This guide was made with you in mind. I know you have dreams and goals, but feel overwhelmed with how to make them happen. In this book I will teach you how to live out the best life simply by setting and reaching your goals. All you need now is to have a plan in place and the dedication to make it happen. As Earl Nightingale said "People with goals succeed because they know where they are going. It's as simple as that."

Let me teach you how to succeed……..

Table of Contents

Foreword 9
Intro 11
What is goal setting? 13
Types of Goals 19
Conquering Your Habits 25
Overcoming fear 31
The Golden Rule to Goal Setting 41
Dream BIG 47
Steps to reaching your goals 53
Maintain your goals 71
Quitting Your Goals 75
Conclusion 79
Appendix A: Reflection Journal 85
Appendix B: Goal Setting Guide 91

Foreword

By Nik Carson

"And the day came when the risk to remain tight in a bud was more painful than the risk it took to blossom"

~Anias Nin

This is the quote that changed everything for me. When I first read it, it seemed like some sort of deep, mysterious, dark message that required years of research in order to understand it. Then one day as I was going through my daily routine of trying to figure out this entrepreneurial life, it hit me! I have got to get out of my own way! I was self-sabotaging in ways that I didn't even realize. I would compare myself and my business with other authors and coaches thinking that I should run my business like theirs because on the outside looking in, they were successful. My books should read that way because their books are on the "Best-Sellers" list. By making these comparisons, it caused me to become stuck and stagnant. I thought I was limited in my abilities to succeed as an author and entrepreneur.

I had been through so many ups and downs. Gains and Losses. High level positions and layoffs! And God knows the list goes on. I remember one day while sitting at my desk staring at the company logo bouncing around on my computer screen, I said to myself, "there has got to be more to my life than this." Don't get me wrong. I was grateful to have a job. But that was it. Just another job. I knew there was something more for me to do. And it wasn't sitting behind someone's desk. At that moment I was ready to start making moves and do the things I had dreamt of doing for several years, because enough was enough.

See, I believe that God gives us dreams, visions, goals, and the desire to want more and move from our comfort zones not only for His Glory, but for one another. To support and build up one another so we all may fulfil the purpose that God has for us. Here is a little hint on how one will know that the dream or vision they have been tossing around and putting off for years is God sent. When the thought of you actually living out your dreams and reaching your goals seems absolutely impossible to be made a reality based on your present surroundings, situation, education or social status! And no matter how many times you try to ignore it, you keep seeing bits and pieces of what your life could look like if you would just act on your dreams and goals!

I am a living testimony that if you step out your comfort zone to follow your dreams and remove the limits fear and insecurity, you will know what it feels like to no longer remain TIGHT IN A BUD!

Being a "Goal Getter" is what perfectly describes my dear friend and fellow author, Nicolya Williams! The information and wisdom she shares in the following pages, will move you into making the decision to not be afraid of your dreams. They are for you to obtain. And here is the guide to do just that!!

It is an honor and privilege to witness and be an active participant in this movement, Nicolya!

Nichole "Nik" Carson
Author of *Be Bold, Blessed, and Beautiful. Principles to Living a Limitless Lifestyle with Confidence and Courage*

Intro

"What is a goal without a plan? It's a wish."
- Antoine De Saint-Exupery

Setting goals is an integral part of your personal development journey. Personal development is the belief that you are worth the effort time and energy needed to develop yourself. This book is for women who are tired of setting goals, but feeling like they never come to fruition. It's time to make your goals your reality and I am ready to help you make that happen! This book will help you work harder not smarter.

Eddie Harris Junior says "The sooner you step out of your comfort zone, the sooner you will recognize that it really wasn't all that comfortable." This is an impressive quote because it is simple, yet true. We often rationalize being in our comfort zones because it feels "safe", when in actuality we are stuck. In our zone of comfort we are not allowing for true growth and it prevents us from reaching our greatest potential.

Can you think for a moment about a situation in your life where you have remained complacent in your comfort zone? What is the reason that you have stayed there? Is it fear, insecurity, doubt, uncertainty? Many people, including myself, have been stuck in comfort zones, and that limit has prevented true growth. I want to help you move past that in order to reach your greatest potential. Studies have shown that we make conscious choices only 5% of the time. The other 95% represents just doing things from habit. To give you some insight, once you have identified small changes it is time to step into the major changes that will propel you in the direction of your dreams. It is time to demolish your comfort zone for good.

Take some time to reflect on these questions:

1. What is the purpose of my comfort zone?
2. What has staying in my comfort zone cost me?
3. What is it that I really want for my life?

This book will help you to recognize your own patterns that keep you limited and stuck. This book will teach you to take consistent action to create better results and reach your goals. It will help you create healthy life habits and appropriate boundaries.

What is goal setting?

"First you jump off the cliff and build your wings on the way down."
- Ray Bradbury

My name is Nicolya Williams. Just like you, I had thousands of goals that I desired to reach, but every last one of them felt so farfetched. I set a goal to eat healthy and within hours I would see a cheesecake and change my mind. I set financial goals to stay debt free, but it seemed like there was always a new emergency forcing me to use my credit card. Needless to say all of these goals that I wasn't reaching truly discouraged me. I spent a year giving up on setting goals and saying that I would let things happen as they happened. When I made that choice, things were happening in my life for sure, but they were not things that I was proud of. In fact it was the exact opposite. Things seemed to be going very wrong. That's when I knew that it was time to make some changes. I knew that immediately I was going to have to start making goal setting and action taking my priorities. I knew I needed to be proactive and could no longer allow being reactive a habit.

So, I set out on a goal setting journey. First I began by setting small goals such as going to bed at 8:30 PM every single night. Next, I started to set even bigger goals such as removing meat from my diet once a week. Then the goals got even bigger. The one thing I came to see was when I was reaching the small goals the medium and the large gold didn't seem that tough. I felt like I could actually do it. For once in a lifetime it felt like my confidence had finally risen. I believe that had a lot to do with the fact that I started off with minor goals and accomplished them. This gave me the momentum and drive to try something even bigger.

When I realized that this wasn't working for me I felt like everybody needed to know the power of goal setting. I wanted to share with the whole world but this was years ago before I even had my business. It was before I felt like my story even mattered. So I just continued to implement the strategies for the goal I was working towards. Sometimes the goals would be personal goals or financial goals. Sometimes I would set academic goals and sometimes I would set parenting goals. This gave me a lot of practice with goal setting. Sometimes I would fail, but I never changed the goal I would instead change the path to reach the goal. One day the idea dropped into my spirit to share my story to people all around the world. I wanted to women all around the world to feel empowered, to feel confident; to feel inspired by the fact that they could not only set goals but they could actually reach them. So buckle up and get ready for this ride!

It's going to be well worth it and I can't wait to see you on the other side.

So what exactly is goal setting? I mean you can write down your goal but what does that mean really? The true definition of **goal setting** is the process by which you identify something that you want to accomplish. Next you establish measurable **goals** and timeframes.

Notice there are three parts to that. One part is setting the goal, the second part is creating a plan and the third part is working to accomplish it. Many people are able to set goals, but it is the lack of planning and execution that trips us up and can keep us stuck. In this book I will help you to create a practical plan that perfectly fits your life and your goal.

There was a study done in 1979 at Harvard where they interviewed their Masters of Business graduate candidates. Out of this class only three percent had written goals, eighty four percent had no goals, and thirteen percent had goals, but they were not written. Ten years later they followed up with these same students and the results were astounding! The three percent who had clear, written goals were earning, on average, ten times more than the other ninety-seven percent combined. Imagine that? Setting goals increased their financial success by ten percent! If this study doesn't highlight the importance of having written goals I don't know what will! When I learned about this study I was completely sold on the power of goal setting and promised that I would continue to not only set my goals, but also create a thorough plan and diligently take action.

Take a moment to ask yourself: When was the last time you wrote down your goals? I don't mean what you posted on Facebook on New Year's. I mean, when was the last time you wrote down your goals and the process it would take to get them accomplished? Don't be embarrassed if you haven't because unfortunately most people don't. The purpose of *The Goal Getter Guide* is to help you live out the life that you truly desire to live. Are you ready to set goals and really achieve them?

You are here because you want to become everything you imagine, you want to earn the respect and esteem of other people, and you want to accomplish your dreams and live up to your potential. In order for that to happen you have to set goals, and more than that you have to actually work to reach them. Without goal setting you can never be successful.

Goal setting is not something that comes natural to us. It is something that must be learned and then practiced. Much like a muscle it is something that has to be built through practice. Through trial and error, I learned a system that I now use for my personal goal setting as well as my clients goals. Not only will I explain the planning process, but I will highlight the background of why it is important in the first place. This process has changed lives and I believe it can do the same for you.

Reflection

How have you set goals in the past?

Did this work for you?

What do you believe to be the purpose of goal setting?

Do you believe that goal setting is important?

What are you hoping to learn from this book?

Types of Goals

"Most people overestimate what they can do in one year and underestimate what they can do in ten years."
- Bill Gates

Before we go into the different types of goals, I want to discuss the number of goals you set. I often work with women who have fifteen to twenty goals in their planner or on their minds. While being determined to accomplish things in your life is great, overwhelming yourself with a lengthy goal list will not help. When you are setting goals I recommend that you pick between 2-3 goals. Obviously each day you set small goals on your daily task list (i.e. make sure I call the dentist to schedule an appointment or be sure to stop by target to get the gift card for my secretary). As far as BIG goals I never recommend setting more than three at a time. The reason for this is because when you set multiple goals you spread yourself thin.

When you set new goals think about all the conflicts that might arise. What's going to suffer because you're prioritizing this new goal or habit? Do you need to prioritize existing goals over this new one? This causes a major conflict of interest because all of your goals feel important, but you can't make time for each of them evenly without one lacking something. Say you want to eat healthy, build your financial savings, get married and start a business. When you are starting a business it is going to take a ton of time away from what you would normally spend on finding new recipes and cooking healthy meals. It may also take a lot of your time up so now you are ordering take out instead of cooking the healthy meals. This is impacting both your health and your budget. On top of that, the time spent looking for a house is stealing time away from your business. This means you are not taking the time you need to set yourself up for success. It truly pays to **take a step back** and reassess whether your goals will conflict. If so, pick the one that is most important and prioritize it. Otherwise, you'll find your brain subconsciously sorting your goals and I promise you will not be happy with the results.

Once you have a handle on certain goals you can begin to add in new goals. For example my aunt and uncle set out to become vegan. They dedicated almost a year to this goal. The reason they dedicated so long was because they needed to change their schedule around to make time for things that were involved with this goal. They needed time for cooking to fit in their schedule, meal planning and grocery shopping. They needed to change their budget around to ensure that they could afford the food that they wanted to buy. Once they had a full grasp on that goal and it became part of their everyday life, they were able to implement new goals. I did the same. I set a goal to meditate for ten minutes per day. Now I do it with very little effort because it has become a part of my life. This is no longer a goal I set because it became a habit. This is one of the benefits of goal setting. You may develop and gain new habits as a result of disciplining yourself in order to meet your goals.

I am not judging you if you have thirty goals. In fact I can relate. About two years ago I was starting two businesses, decluttering my house, working, going through a divorce and in graduate school. I thought I would be able to handle all of these things and I was very WRONG! Each part of my life was suffering just a little because I was dedicating minimal amounts of time to each. In reality if I had focused on two at a time I could have handled those in a more efficient manner and in less time then move on to the next goal. Do not beat yourself up if you have a lot of goals. The truth is that your will to have many goals shows you care to make a good life for yourself. Now that you know that this does not work, I challenge you to choose two to three goals that you can really dedicate yourself to.

The first thing you want to do is to understand what type of goal you are setting. There are so many different types of goals and in this chapter we will review them. This will help you when you are going forward in creating a plan. Let's identify the type of goals as it relates to time frames.

Lifetime goals are goals that can take ten or more years to achieve. To think of your lifetime goals, visualize where you would like to be in fifteen years. Where are you living? What is your family structure? What is your money situation? Answering these questions will help you to identify what type of goals you should be setting. Since you are always growing it is important to reflect on these goals every two years or so to ensure that they are still in alignment with what you desire for your future.

Long Term Goals are goals that take approximately five to ten years to reach. Similar to life time goals, you can visualize what you want the next ten years to look like and start writing goals that align with that. These goals should also be reviewed regularly to ensure that you are still working on the correct things. Ten years ago

I would have never had a desire to start my own business, today I love my business so trust me when I say long term goals can change rapidly.

Short term goals vary in time length. They may be a month, six months or even a year. These are goals that are stepping stones, with the purpose of reaching long term or lifetime goals. An example of a short term goal would be to pay off a credit card balance 3of $1000. This could align with your lifetime goal of being completely debt free.

There are other types of goals that you can set as it relates to the various areas in your life.

Career Goals relate to aspirations for your growth in relation to your career. This could be to get a promotion, earn a raise or make more money for your company, etc.

Financial Goals are set to make some major changes to your finances. This could be to pay off your debt, buy a home, or to make a large purchase.

Personal Development Goals- These are goals that help you to do things that align with your potential. This could include increasing your reading, writing a book, learn a new skill or to travel to a new place. These are my favorite goals, but they are also the goals that are rarely set. Many people overlook the process of improving themselves. Personal development goals help you to be successful in your other goals. For example when I was beginning my career as a guidance counselor I set a personal development goal of attending a conference once a year to sharpen my skills. This aligned with my overall goal of being an effective leader in my school building for my students.

Spiritual goals relate to your spiritual growth. This could be goals such as attending church more regularly, joining a small group, meditating daily or reading the bible. This goal will help you stay centered and reflective on the things that are happening in your day to day life. I set spiritual goals regularly and then make them a part of my life. For example I set a goal of finding a small group for support in my church. I attended a few, found one I loved and now I go every Friday. This was one of the best goals I have ever set, because I have been connected with some powerful people.

Educational Goals often crossover with personal development and career goals. But mostly your educational goals after college will deal with specific things you need for your education/career/job/future job. These can be goals such as attending conferences, going to college or getting a new certification or license.

Relationship goals are set with the intention of improving your relationships. These goals can be to go on a date night once per week, have children, get married etc.

Physical or Health Goals are related to your body and your health. These include goals such as eating healthy, becoming vegetarian, have a regular exercise routine or keep vital signs within a healthy range.

Decide what you want in every area of your life. After all you can't hit a target that doesn't exist right?! I am sure you may feel overwhelmed with all of the choices and that is completely normal. Just take a moment and start to think about what things you are desiring to accomplish. Now, highlight which category they fit into.

<u>Reflection</u>

What are my three biggest goals?

Why did I choose these goals for myself?

How many different types of goals have I set?

What are the outcomes I desire with these goals?

How do each of these goals benefit me?

Conquering Your Habits

"The secret to breaking a bad habit is to love something greater than the habit."
- Bryant McGill

One of my favorite quotes is "Do what is right, not what is easy." This quote can be applied to many situations but as we discuss habits I think it especially applies. I know that the choices that we make are often the easy choices. They are what is comfortable and what we are used to. They provide us with peace and security because we have become familiar with them. The truth is they also keep us limited or stuck and they keep us from growing and reaching our potential. This is why it is important to do what is right. When we identify a habit we need to begin or a habit that we need to break it is usually because we know it is the right thing to do.

When we do the right thing there are a number of results that could follow. Growth, inspiring others, reaching goals that seemed too farfetched and impressing ourselves and other people are a few. The quality of your life is definitely created by your habits. Most people with high energy make daily choices to rest and nourish their body with healthy foods and water. People who are rich often spend time investing in their understanding of money as well as their businesses. The most intelligent people spend time reading and learning. Their life quality is determined by the choices that they make.

So what exactly is a habit? The word *habit* is defined as a regular practice that is difficult to break or difficult to begin. How many times have you identified a habit that you want to break or a habit that you want to begin and failed miserably? It happens to the best of us. Think of New Years for example. Every year the ENTIRE world makes New Year's resolutions. We decide that we will eat healthy, or that we will read more, or that we will give up smoking or cussing or whatever other resolutions we may create. But within a few weeks those resolutions are tossed out of the window and all of those statuses about this being "my year" are changed to "someday I will get better".

After working with many women, I have concluded that the biggest reason they cannot accomplish their goals is the fact that they struggle with nasty habits that impact the process negatively. Sometimes our habits are obvious, such as spending a lot of money on fast food. Other times our habits are not so evident such as checking your Facebook likes and getting stuck in the social media black hole. On the flip side, women struggle with implementing habits that put them in a position to succeed as it relates to their goals. I am here to share a strategy that has worked for many women including myself in order to break the habits that prevent you from reaching your goals. I agree with Marie Forleo when she says that "Success does not come from what you do occasionally. It comes from what you do consistently". So let's make your consistent actions the ones that will help you succeed at reaching your goals.

We've all got the same twenty-four hours in a day, which totals one hundred and sixty eight hours in a week. We have to protect it. One of the biggest things I hear women say is that they cut down on their sleep to make time to work on their goals. Since we only have 168 hours in a week, the time we take to sleep, exercise, or and eat might seem like a time sucker but without taking time to take care of our bodies we are sure to fail.

In order to be effective at working on your goals you must be sure to restore your body and boost your physical energy. Getting adequate sleep gives you the opportunity to restore and refresh your body so that you can make choices with a clear head. It also allows you to stay sharp when having to deal with tough situations. Sleep also refreshes our emotional state of mind by decreasing irritability, or sadness. Lastly, sleep revitalizes our bodies which reduces depression, fatigue and stress.

To sum this up if you want to reach your goals you can't ditch sleep. To ensure that you're getting a good night's sleep, it must include both quality and quantity. To ensure that you are including both aspects set a regular bedtime and stick with it. Turn off all of your screens in advance and avoid late-day exercise. Kill all the lights and keep the temperature low. This sets you up for successful sleep and in turn helps you with working towards your goals effectively.

Have you ever heard the saying "Show me your routines, habits and rituals and I will show you your future?" Our life is truly determined by our habits. Take a minute and ask yourself what do your habits say about you? Your habits, routines and rituals ultimately determine your destiny! Your life won't change unless you actually change. You have to start by being more disciplined and taking control of your habits! The truth is that our habits and choices compound. If you choose to eat unhealthy for one day it doesn't really hurt, but if you do it for several weeks then the impact is huge! If you chose to drink 64 ounces of water for one day that's nice but if you do it every day for a year then the impact it has on your health is phenomenal.

This is why it is imperative that you stay on top of your habits. You want the compound effect to work in your favor not against you! If you change your habits once in a blue moon don't be upset when you only see the results once in a blue moon! We are our own worst enemies when it comes to staying focused. The trouble is that there will always be temptations, but we have to learn how to get out of our own way. There is a 7 step process that I use to break free from the negative habits and to propel myself in the direction of my dreams.

1. **Identify** what habit you want to break or what habit you want to begin. It is important to identify habits that you want to practice that will in turn increase and lead to the results you desire.

2. **Know your "why".** Why did you start making this choice or why is this a habit that you want to begin? Are you doing this for your business? For your finances? For your family? For your health? To support someone else? This step is extremely important. If your why is not strong enough then you will not succeed. It has to be something that you desire. For example my daughter was having horrible reactions to dairy products. For this reason I have removed milk from my diet. It was hard, but I could not see her struggle any longer. That was extremely important to me. I still eat cheese, but who knows that may change soon too…baby steps right? I tried to give up milk in the past, but truthfully I was not sold on the idea because my "why" was not strong enough. Now it is!

3. **Choose to begin today.** When we continue to push off our goals we send signals to our subconscious mind stating that it is okay to not work towards what we want or that our goals and desires are not significant. Many times I work with women who have been putting off their goals for several years. When I ask them why they waited so long they admit that they always thought they had time. I call this the "Someday mindset." This is where you assume that you have more time in the world so you make comments such as "I will get to that eventually" or "someday I will have time for that". Do not get caught up in that state of mind, I promise it will not get you anywhere. All it is doing is slowing you down and preventing you from reaching your goals.

4. **Believe that you can**. Like the old saying "Whether you believe you can or you can't, you are probably right". The truth is, our belief system impacts our actions. When you believe in yourself and your ability to achieve what you desire, you become unstoppable.

5. **Be accountable.** Identify a person that can be there to support you with ending or beginning a new habit. Create an inner circle of people who you can share your goals with and get feedback and support to help push you forward. Consider hiring a life coach to work with you through the process of working through your goals and overcoming nasty habits that prevent your success. A good life coach can help you examine what you truly want from life, and the impact that your daily choices have on these goals. They can also help to hold you accountable. When you have someone that holds you accountable you increase the chances of following through.

6. **Give yourself grace.** This was the hardest step for me because I struggle with perfectionism. Some things come really easy to me but one habit that I have diligently been working on breaking is buying takeout food. Every time I fell back into that habit I would beat myself up. This only sent me into a downward spiral and made me feel like I wasn't good enough to stop this habit. I would solve it by repeating the habit.

7. **Visualize the rewards!** When we practice visualization we are able to overcome challenges that we have when trying to implement change. Take time each day to visualize what your life will look like when you make these desired changes. Will you be healthier? Happier? More in shape? More financially stable? What will that look like for you? The more vivid you make this vision the more you will feel excited to actually achieve it. Some experts believe that when you visualize your goals, you can stir up different emotions that pull you into alignment with that vision. This is why vision boards have become so popular. If you have not created one I highly recommend it. A lot of times we are focused on all of the ways our habits have negatively impacted us and the problems that they have caused. I plead with you today to be led by your dreams not pushed by your problems.

Beginning something new (whether that is starting a new habit or getting rid of an old one) is challenging. There will be days where you succeed, there will be days where you fail. The key is to

NOT quit. When you keep pushing through, you are telling yourself that this is a priority and it makes the work more worthwhile. This is what I call the winners strategy. Winners do not focus on their failures they focus on what they can do to get better. I would like to encourage you by sharing that the struggle with beginning something new is only temporary. If you keep that in mind you will be able to push through to the other side. You will be grateful that you challenged yourself.

Here is an affirmative statement I say to remind myself often why getting in control of my habits is important:

My habits lead to goal achievement.

My decisions determine my ability to achieve my goals. I practice habits that build me and make me successful.

I spend a lot of time reading because it produces knowledge and awareness about my goals. Professional opportunities are more attainable when I am aware. Keeping abreast of the news allows me to prepare myself for global change.

Exercise clears my mind and allows me to focus on work. When I release the stress of yesterday, I am able to concentrate on resolving the challenges of today.

Balance is essential to coping with competing aspects of my life. Although I like to get things done quickly, I am diligent about making time for relaxation.

A body that is relaxed feels ready to take on the world.

Scheduling time for study is easy for me because I focus on my upcoming graduation day. Zoning in on the mission at hand ignites the desire to put first things first.

Today, I practice positive habits that help me achieve my goals. I realize that taking this approach results in less difficulty in my life. Goals are more straightforward and simpler to achieve when I put myself in the position to achieve them.

Overcoming fear

"Many of us are not living our dreams because we are too busy living our fears."
- Les Brown

Fear is the number one factor that can prevent us from setting BIG goals and going after them. Fear is our body's response to potential danger. Nobody should be stuck living in fear. Fear can be our ally or it can be our enemy. Fear is part instinct, part learned, and part taught. An example of an instinctive fear is pain. We naturally respond to pain with fear. For example I went to the doctor a few weeks ago for severe back pain. I was fearful of the outcome because the pain was so strong.

Learned fears are the result of being taught to be afraid of different people or places. If you burned yourself on the stove that experience has taught you to be fearful of going near the stove. Or maybe you almost drowned as a child and now you are fearful of water.

Sometimes fear is even imagined. We may get scared because of what we think could happen. Harmless events can seem scary when you are dealing with preconceived fear. For example, when I walk into my garden, I begin to feel fear because I think I will see spiders. I then have a very strong reaction to every little bug that goes by me. Another example would be if you were afraid of flying. Even the slightest turbulence would push your blood pressure through the roof of the plane.

Fear can have an impact on our lives. Have you ever heard of fight or freeze? Freeze means you stop what you are doing and focus on the fearful stimulus to decide what to do next. This is what I call stuck. Fear can put us in situations where we feel hopeless to move. People who stay here often obsess about their situation or they complain, but they never move or take action. When you respond in this manner it leads to the feeling of being stuck or hopeless, and could potentially lead to depression.

When you respond to fear with a fight reaction you begin to take action against your fear. You may challenge yourself to step outside of your comfort zone or you may try something you were once afraid of. When you have the fight response you identify the threat and you jump into action immediately and without flinching.

Okay…so take a moment to think about your fears. They are coming from a place of wanting to avoid failure or humiliation to some extent. There are many reasons people feel fear. These reasons include fear of failure, fear of success, fear of being talked about or fear of rejection.

Let's discuss each of these fears and how they impact you.

Fear of Success

So the first fear I will discuss is the fear of success. This one is usually most shocking to others. People think, "Why in the world would you NOT want to be successful? Why would you not want money, and the nice house and the flourishing business?" When working with women who have battled with this, it really helped me to reflect on why women may feel fearful upon accomplishing things or even with the potential of success.

We aren't afraid of success in itself. We are afraid of what is required to get to that success. Many times this means we are afraid to sacrifice, get uncomfortable, work hard, and the commitment. We fear that we won't be able to live up to the requirements and therefore we would fall short of our dreams. The truth about this fear is that we aren't scared of the success, we are scared of the things that come with it.

Another component of this is that many people fear that once they achieve success they will not necessarily be able to maintain it. This puts pressure on the individual to be perfect. I personally deal with this in my business. I am doing well and would like to be able to help and empower as many as women as possible. This sometimes scares me because I contemplate on what would happen if I do get so many clients that I am overwhelmed. The key to maintaining success is maintaining the consistency and dedication that got you to the place that you're in.

One strategy I use with clients as well as in my personal life is to define what success looks like. This covers the area of business, relationships, money etc. I had a client that was not sure what success was supposed to look like and that is why she was fearful because she had never clearly defined it. It is important to understand that success is unique to who you are and your life circumstances. No one can define success for you. If I feel like I should be as successful as Michelle Obama, then I may fear success because her role is huge. This may not be my version of success. If I am able to define it then I know what is best for me.

Here are three signs that you may struggle with fear of success:

1. You often come up with excuses to distract you from completing tasks to reach your goals

2. You always compare your goals and success to other people that are better than you, and this makes you feel that your efforts are worthless.

3. You often try to downplay accomplishments.

Failure is the second thing that women fear. I honestly think that each of us feel this at some point in our lives. I always think of the quote "Failure is the opportunity to begin again". If we spend our time seeing failure as something bad then we will always live in a state of fear. If we in turn realize that failure is something that helps us grow, we are less likely to become paralyzed as a result of our fear. Failure should really be looked at as a learning opportunity. If we are honest with ourselves, we can reflect on the circumstances and learn from those situations each time we fail.

Fear of failure can cause us to be paralyzed. When we feel this way we don't really put forth much effort or we don't try at all. It is obvious that our heart is not in it. For example we may set a goal of saving $1,000 by the end of the year. But when we fail to reach the half-way mark we see it as failure and then stop putting in efforts. When instead we should take a moment to reflect and identify what things prevented us from reaching those goals and then learn from those situations.

Take a moment to define what failure means. Does failure mean that you don't make as much money as you want or something did not turn out the way you envisioned? The truth is, these things happened the way they did in order for us to learn from the experience. When you reflect on what true failure looks like, you may realize that you did not actually fail. And if you still don't agree, ask yourself what is the worst thing that can happen if you do fail? You can start again whatever it may be.

I personally battled with fear of failure. I have wanted to start a coaching business since 2012. I spent so many years living in fear. I would always say things like "I've never been an entrepreneur so I don't know how to be one." or "No one is going to listen to me."

This kept me paralyzed although I believe my true calling is to inspire and motivate women. I could be so much farther in my business, had I not stood still holding on to fear.

Fear of Failure
Five signs that you might be scared of failure:

1. Worrying about what other people think about you.

2. Worrying about your ability to pursue the future you desire.

3. Worrying about how smart or capable you are.

4. Worrying about disappointing people whose opinion you value.

5. The tendency to tell people beforehand that you don't expect to succeed in order to lower their expectations.

Fear of Criticism
This is the fear of being talked about. This is often where the fear of failure and success stems from. The truth is we can't consume ourselves with what people think about us. Most of the time they don't even know what they think of themselves. People will ALWAYS have something to say about you. Give them something to talk about. Let them talk about your efforts, your confidence, etc. Do not let other people keep you bound in fear and allowing them to let you live limited. We can't control what others think about us and when you become consumed with those thoughts it negatively impacts your life. Take a moment and ask yourself who are you trying to please and why? You have to know that you cannot make everyone happy with what you do. Someone will always have an issue with it. I have learned to focus on pleasing God.

Here are signs that you are scared of what others think:
1. You are not being authentically you. Instead you try to fit a mold of what you think others think you should be. You wear masks- you change your identity based on your location. Yes we do need to have some change but you still should hold true to who you

really are. When you free yourself from the fear of what others think, you're brave enough to be yourself.

2. You apologize for things you like and for being you. You should never have to apologize simply for being yourself.

3. You are always thinking about what other people think about you.

Fear of Rejection

The last fear that I would like to mention is the fear of rejection. Although I believe it is important to highlight this fear, I won't write too long about it because most of the women I work with battle with fear in the other three realms.

Fear of rejection often stems from rejection dealt with from people in our past. This fear can be especially present when you are setting career goals or relationship goals because it involves others approval or participation. This then makes us feel like people in our life currently will also reject us. When people do not agree with us this does not mean that they will reject us. So you have to remember that people are different and that is okay. This does not equal rejection. Yes, rejection does happen, but it all works out for our good. Rejection is for our protection. Rejection one way opens the door to something better.

Here are signs that you fear rejection:

1. You are easily offended.
2. You often feel like you are not good enough when it comes to accomplishing goals.

Fear is not an emotion that is isolated. Along with fear you can feel excitement, disappointment and many other emotions. Fear is also not something that is unique to only you. I have worked with thousands of children and several hundred women and we all deal with fear to some extent. Now that we have acknowledged fear and how it negatively impacts our goal setting and our ambition, the question is how can we fix this?

Listed below are the steps that you can take to conquer your fear:

1. First identify what fear you are battling with. Once you identify this, take some time to reflect on your fear. What is the root of fear? Some people feel fear because they have been talked about in the past, or people told them they will fail, or maybe because they saw people fail. Ask yourself why do I feel this fear? Really dig into that "why". Do not try to sugar coat the answer to appease yourself or anyone else. Without truly opening your mind up to why, you will likely stay stuck in the place of fear that you are currently trying to break free from.

2. Next, identify all of the things that fear has kept you from accomplishing. Has it kept you from changing your jobs, starting a business, writing your book, going to work out? What ways have fear kept you from moving forward? When I did this part of the process I found myself being upset with my fear and I was ready to fight it. I was so upset because I could have written many books by now had I not let fear tell me I couldn't. The time of reflection truly upset me because I realized that being consumed in fear changed my whole life and not in a way that I desired.

3. After this processing time you want to challenge your thoughts. People who believe that everything they think is right, and never question their assumptions make life harder for themselves. We are our own worst enemy at times and so we have to remember this when those negative thoughts come in. Every thought that comes into your mind that is negative must be rebutted with positive thoughts. Oftentimes fear causes us to assume that the worst thing will happen. What if what you are thinking will never come true? What if what you are thinking is wrong? Start to challenge that negative thinking with those questions.

4. We attract what we think about, so if you spend all your time thinking about the potential fear you will indeed attract fearful circumstances. So, spend your time practicing how you want to feel. Spend your time reflecting and thinking on the things that bring you happiness and joy. If you want to feel happy, practice being happy. If you want to be confident practice being confident. Think about it like this: If you want to learn to swim, but instead you spend all of your time thinking about how stupid swimming is and how you will

never learn to swim, you will begin to internalize this, therefore you will never learn to swim successfully. But if you approach swimming with a positive or confident attitude, learning to swim will come more naturally. After all we attract what we think about, so if you spend all your time thinking about fearful circumstances, you will attract them.

5. Cover fearful thoughts with gratitude. This step is my favorite because when you are busy being grateful you have no time to feel angry or fearful. When you feel like people are judging you, be grateful that you are doing so well that they have something to talk about. When you are fearful that you will fail, be grateful for your confidence to try. When you're fearful of success, be grateful for opportunity. Literally switch to gratitude and you will feel better. Trust me, I have to do this often and it takes time for it to become a habit, but it works very well.

6. Next identify a group of people that can be there to support you. When you have no way to express your fears they begin to bottle up and they can consume you. Make an inner circle of people who you can share your fears with and get feedback and support to help push you forward. Consider hiring a life coach to work with you through the process of working through your fears. A good life coach can help you examine what you truly want from life, and where your fears come from. I personally have a coach that I use to help me when I am stepping into a new territory with my business. She is amazing because I am able to step out of my comfort zone without letting fear stop me.

7. The last step is to take action. This is probably the most important step because you can go through all of the previous steps to work through fear but if you stop at step six, all you did was reflect. You have not pushed yourself away from the fear. Let's call a spade a spade – fear is fear and nothing more. They are created by your imagination and they make reality seem more scary or overwhelming than it truly is. When you take action and face your fears, they become weaker, because you realize that reality isn't nearly as bad as your imagination.

You can conquer your fear. I know this because I did and it changed my life. Now it's time to change yours.

Reflection

What fear am I dealing with most at the moment? (You can list more than one)?

How does the fear make me feel?

How has fear manifested itself in my life?

In what ways has fear kept me stuck or stagnant?

Has there been a time in the past where I battled with fear? When I overcame it what was the outcome?

What steps will I take to conquer my fear?

The Golden Rule to Goal Setting

"If you want to be happy, set a goal that commands your thoughts, liberates your energy and inspires your hopes."
Andrew Carnegie

When setting goals I have one acronym that I follow very closely. I call it my golden goal setting rule. If my goal does not align with this then it is pointless to me and it will likely not be reached. The acronym is as follows:

G- Get excited about your goal
O- Open up your schedule
A- Allow for support and accountability
L- Loyalty needs to last

So let me break it down! When you're setting your goals you must be excited about them. If you are just working on them because someone told you to, you will never be dedicated to your goals in a real way that makes a difference. How many times have you set a goal because someone told you that you had to accomplish it? Maybe you went to college and picked your major because your mother told you that is what you needed to do. Maybe you chose a job to impress your friends. Think about how that feels? It is not truly exciting to work at a goal just because someone else wants you to. When you are setting goals it should be something that excites you. Something that keeps you up at night and wakes you up early the next morning. When you are excited about it you are more inclined to work diligently on your goal. I know when I first started my business I did not make one dollar during my first six months and I had invested almost $9,000. For most people that would have been enough to throw in the towel, but for me it was not. My business kept me motivated. I felt excited with the thoughts of working on my business and all of the women that I would be able to impact. I was not making an impact yet but the thought of it was enough. I did not care how much time or money I was putting in I was still excited about my goal. I still maintained the same passion from when I began. Trust me, that excitement motivated me when the process was very overwhelming and discouraging.

The second part of the golden goal setting acronym is to open up your schedule. When you are working on your goals you must open up your schedule. The goals won't automatically fit into your schedule. You must carve out the necessary time and make it nonnegotiable. This means that when things threaten to stop you from working on your goal you must put those things in their place. I remember when I began writing this book. I was challenged by so many different distractions. I was going through a very contentious divorce, my skin care business was not doing well, my daughter was in a gifted program at school which required extra work, and my youngest started a pre-school with where she was actually assigned homework. Let's not even mention that I was in school full time myself. I was busy and very stressed out. My emotions got the best of me and I allowed myself to believe that working on my goals was too big of a task. I wanted to just lay in bed and forget about all that I needed to do. I had to challenge those thoughts. One great strategy I used was an hour of power. This is where I scheduled one hour blocks on my schedule to work on my goals. I told myself that if I could at least give one dedicated non interrupted hour per day then I would be able to accomplish my goal in no time. While this book took much longer than any of my other books I know that my power hours made all of the difference.

    The third part of the golden goal setting rule is to allow for accountability and support. Have you ever heard the saying "Move in silence"? This means to avoid announcing your goal. I love this idea, because you shouldn't announce your goal to the world. However, there is something to be said about having some accountability with your goal. I always tell my clients that there is no goal worth achieving in isolation. When you set goals they should be done with others in mind. Maybe it is to help earn extra money to take your kids on the extra vacation. Maybe it is to start a business to help other women. In order to reach those goals, start thinking of people that can help support you. When you try to reach a goal in isolation it can be very frustrating. It can be lonely working on goals in general, but when you have someone to call to discuss it with, it takes the pressure off your shoulders. That is why it is important to have people in your corner that can help motivate, encourage, inspire and even mentor you. Those people truly come in handy when you feel like throwing in the towel and giving up on the goal. A mentor can help to give you steps and suggestions so that the process is not nearly as overwhelming. Find someone who you trust and will help to hold you accountable during your process. It will be worth it in the long run.

When I began my business I told three people. I told my mother because we spoke every day and I knew that her asking me questions about my business would automatically remind me what I was supposed to be working on. I told a friend who also had a business. Although her business was completely different than mine I knew she would understand the tough parts of the entrepreneurial journey. We spoke bi-weekly. I also hired a business coach. She helped me learn the correct processes to implement to make the process seamless. If I had tried to learn to start an online business all on my own I would have never made one penny I know that without a doubt. There are so many ins and outs to running a business and following the footsteps of someone else was extremely helpful. Honestly, that was probably one of the best investments in my entire life.

Take some time to think about this: You can't ask the neighbors how to get out of the neighborhood. You can't ask broke people how to be rich!! Sooooooo....who are you talking to about your goals? I know you are excited and I know you want to know everything possible! I hate to break it to you, but you can't talk to everybody! You can't take advice from everyone willing to give it!! Stop talking to people who haven't accomplished anything. Surround yourself with like-minded and successful people. Have these people hold you accountable to what you said you would do. When you take this step your progress will be magical!

The fourth step of the golden goal setting process is to be loyal to your goal. Too many times people set goals and then throw in the towel when the process gets too hard. If what you are doing is not working change the plan not the goal. If every time you get frustrated you change the goal I can promise you that will never reach any goals, unless it is by accident. This is why it is so important to get excited and love your goal. Without that passion you will never be dedicated in a way that matters. This is also why you must be loyal to the goal. When you are loyal to your goal, you will make it a priority and put in the necessary work to achieve it.

I share this strategy with you because it has changed my life. I always apply this process to each one of my goals and it really has helped me a ton. I know that when I am working on each of my goals they will manifest in great ways because I put in the work beforehand!

Reflection

G- Get excited about your goal
O- Open up your schedule
A- Allow for support and accountability
L- Loyalty needs to last

What is the goal you are currently working?

G- How do you feel about your goal? How do you know you feel this way?

O- How have you adjusted your schedule to make time for the goal you are working on?

A- Who will support you and hold you accountable as you're working on this goal?

L- How will you ensure that you remain focused and loyal to your goal?

Dream BIG

"The future belongs to those who believe in the beauty of their dreams."
- Eleanor Roosevelt

How many times have you set a goal just to change your mind because it felt too far out of your reach? Maybe it's that dream of a marriage, but you're not even dating. Maybe you set a goal to be debt free, but you owe over $200,000 in student loans. No matter how farfetched the goal is, I am here to tell you that it is still okay to desire the outcome. At the beginning of 2017, my spiritual sister set a goal to pay off her house by the end of the year. She owed $50,000 on it and knew that she would not be able to naturally make this happen, but as she said…she was believing God for a miracle. Ten months later she found that there was an error and they needed to take about $10,000 off. She had also applied $10,000 towards the goal. Although she did not reach the entire monetary amount she was about half way towards hitting her mark. Now, had she turned away from the goal because it felt too overwhelming, I can guarantee she would not even be a fourth of the way to the goal. She proactively paid down the balance by sending in money, making calls, looking into programs, etc.

So, setting large goals does not have to be discouraging. In fact it should encourage you. Dreaming BIG is what got me where I am. I am no fancy English major. I was just a woman with a dream to become an author. I made that my goal, mapped out a plan and made it happen. That's what goals are about. If we looked for everything to be easy or even to make sense no one in the world would accomplish anything.

Take Walt Disney for example. He was fired from his first job because he was told that he lacked imagination. He had 300 banks turn down his Walt Disney theme park idea. At one stage, he was bankrupt. He maintained determination and focused on what he wanted to achieve. Today, his movies, merchandise and theme parks are worth billions. Another example is Michael Jordan. Almost everyone would classify him as the world's best basketball player. During his sophomore year, he failed to make the varsity basketball team due to his height. Michael was 5'11. Based on his height, he was classified as too short to play at a high school level. Jordan didn't make excuses. Instead, he practiced hard perfecting his game. His burning desire to be the best, to persevere, to practice, to do more than the minimum and his refusal to quit eventually led to him being one of the greatest basketball players of all time. How about Oprah Winfrey, one of the women I look up to. She was fired from her evening news reporter gig with Baltimore's WJZ-TV because she got too emotionally invested in her stories. A Baltimore TV producer reportedly told her she was "unfit for television news." She had her own talk show and now her own TV station….Imagine that!

These are stories of people who had every right to give up on their goals. They had every right to not believe in the power of dreaming BIG. But they didn't. Their goals were so important to them that they chose to pursue them even when it was obvious they shouldn't have. This is the state of mind you want to be in to be successful at pursuing your goals. Choose one of these individuals for your inspiration when things are getting too difficult or you are feeling overwhelmed. Remind yourself about their focus, attitude and the fact that they never gave up on their dream.

One factor that I see impact goal setters regularly is indecision. This often comes when we have to narrow down our goals or even develop a plan to start working toward them. Indecisiveness can be the result of a lack of clarity. If you're unclear about your values and your goals, you lack purpose. So many people know they want to be successful, but they have no clue what that means for them. When I work with my clients I ask them to visualize their dream life. I always put emphasis on them being the creator and being sure that there are no limitations on what they include. Now it's your turn to try it:

Imagine that you can make your life perfect! What is happening in your life, what does it look like?

Now you probably started off with great ideas and then part of you said that you were being ridiculous. STOP IT!

If you want to be free to set goals and believe that they can happen you have to grab control over those thoughts that tell you that your goals will never be accomplished.

You see your thoughts are the reflection of mental clutter. This is where it all starts. Get control of your thoughts, and your mental clutter will be tamed. This is a major task, and not for the faint-hearted! It can be done, though. There are several things that affect your thoughts, including:

Mental habits
Everyday stress
Making decisions (especially when there are too many options)
Unfinished business
Grief

The quickest way to reframe those thoughts is to replace every negative thought with a positive alternative. Here are a few examples:

Instead of Saying:	Say This:
"I can't do this."	"Man, this is tough. I am feeling challenged.
"This is too hard."	"This is getting tough. I am going to reach out for help."

In my house we have a rule and it is called the rule of can't. This rule means that we are not allowed to use the word *can't*. I made this rule intentionally because I believe there is so much power in your thoughts and when you're saying words such as can't you are putting limits on yourself and standing in your own way. If we do we have to put $.10 in a jar and we have to immediately replace the word can't with a positive statement of the things that we can do. Since this rule has been implemented it has really changed my life. Our jar was consistently full, but now we rarely fill it up. My girls and I set goals regularly that seem crazy. The most insane part is we actually believe that our dreams and our goals can happen.

Some of the most worthy goals are also the most difficult to achieve. Major accomplishments can take a tremendous amount of time and effort, and it is easy to get discouraged and give up. I am here to tell you that when you push past that initial desire to throw in the towel you will be very pleased with the results. So set BIG goals, work diligently towards what you want, fight through the urge to give up and watch the results! Once you change your thoughts you can change your entire life.

Reflection

What thoughts do you have that interfere with goal setting?

What daily actions negatively interfere with goal setting?

What do you believe about your goals?

Steps to reaching your goals

"So many of our dreams at first seem impossible, then they seem improbable, and then, when we summon the will, they soon become inevitable."
- Christopher Reeve

So far up to this point, we have discussed the history behind our goals and why we should be setting goals in the first place. Now we need to discuss creating and implementing a plan to be successful while working towards goals.

Here are the steps to setting and reaching your goals:

Identify your why

There's only one person in this goal-setting process that matters. You. So what is the reason you are working on this goal. Without having a strong why, you will not work hard at your goal and the outcome will truly reflect that.

Identify the goal. Be SMART about it.

What is the goal that you desire to reach? A lot of people assume that when they set goals stating what it is that they want or stating the actual outcome is the goal itself. That is not the truth. You must identify exactly what the goal is. Your goal should be clear and specific, otherwise you won't be able to focus your efforts or feel truly motivated to achieve it. A specific goal could be, "I want togain the skills and experience necessary to make teacher of the month next month so that I can improve my portfolio and expand my career opportunities"

You have probably heard of **SMART goals** already. But do you apply the rule to your goals? The simple fact is that for goals to be powerful, they should be designed to be SMART. There are many variations of what SMART stands for, but the essence is this – goals should be:

- Specific
- Measurable
- Achievable
- Relevant
- Time Based

Set Specific Goals

Your goal must be clear and well defined. Vague or generalized goals are unhelpful because they don't provide sufficient direction for what you're working on. Remember, the purpose of goals to show you the way, almost like a blueprint. Make it as easy as you can to get where you want to go by defining precisely where you want to end up.

Set Measurable Goals

Include very clear and precise details when setting your goals such as amounts and dates. This will help you to measure your degree of success as you go on. If your goal is simply defined as "To lose weight" how will you know when you have been successful? Is it after five pounds, ten pounds or are you measuring in inches? Without a way to measure your success you miss out on the celebration that comes with knowing you have actually hit the goal.

Set Achievable Goals

Make sure that it's actually possible to achieve the goals you set. If you set a goal that you have no hope of achieving, you will only demoralize yourself and feel like a failure. However, resist the urge to set goals that are too easy. I am a firm believer that a good goal should push you out of your comfort zone and make you a tad bit uncomfortable! By setting realistic yet challenging goals, you hit the balance you need. These are the types of goals that require you to "raise the bar" and they bring the greatest personal satisfaction.

Set Relevant Goals

Set goals that are relevant to what you want to accomplish. Maybe you want to be able to take your family on a HUGE vacation. An example of a relevant goal would be saving money towards that ultimate desire. Don't set a goal to sell your house if you desire to be a homeowner. Make the goal relevant to you and your life goals.

Set Time based Goals

Finally, your goals must have a time frame. Too many times women set goals and have no time frame. They say "I want to lose thirty pounds" but they never say when. This goal can become very frustrating because they never know when they will lose that weight. Now you could change that to "I want to lose thirty pounds by my wedding ". That gives you the date and then you can break the goal down into bite sized chunks so you know how much weight you should be working towards each week.

Every goal needs a target date, so that you have a deadline to focus on and something to work toward. Creating this timeline allows you to set a proper schedule. If you are just up in the air about your timeline it is just as bad as not having a goal. You will have no push to get it done soon. This helps to improve your time management. In order to set a good timeline, you will want to consider the various factors that contribute to the goal. You may need to identify sub goals for the main goal.

For example, if you want ten new clients, a stepping stone goal may be to have a new e-book promotion. Also, you will want to take into consideration how much time you will be able to commit to that goal daily. I was once told that there are no bad goals just timelines. You may have to adjust your timeline according to your goal and that is okay as long as the goal is still obtainable. The key to reach a goal is to work on it every single day!

After working through the SMART process you will want to ensure that you are fully committed to the goal. Without that commitment you will not put forth the effort needed to succeed.

Commit to your goal

You cannot start working on a goal on Tuesday and give up on Thursday. That is not how goals work. The process is long and challenging. This is why dedication is imperative. You have to be dedicated to the outcome, otherwise you won't put in the work to get there. Write down three ways that you will ensure that you maintain the commitment to your goal.

Change your surroundings

Your environment includes your home and work environments. Avoid underestimating the impact your environment can have on your mental clutter. Removing environmental clutter can have a positive effect on the clutter between your ears. Create an environment that is conducive to your success. Sometimes this means leaving your house to work on your goals. Other times this means creating a place in your house where you can be productive.

Surround yourself with the right people
It is rare to have people that truly want to see you excel. However, that's no reason to tolerate those who intentionally become obstacles in your life. If it's a close friend or family member, first have a frank discussion. If that fails to have an effect, then show them the door.
1. Friends from another time. It might be an old college friend or a co-worker from 20 years ago. Do you have anything in common besides a past? How much enjoyment do you receive from them? Think about it and make the necessary adjustments.
2. Unfamiliar social media pals. You know these people. They're Facebook "friends" that are actually friends of friends of friends. Do you need to see the birthday pictures of their grandchildren?
3. If you're using social media to promote your business, the more the merrier. Otherwise, make the necessary cuts.
4. Think about the people at work. You have fewer options here. You might be able to eliminate those troubling people that work for you, but even that's not easy in today's day and age. You can find another position within the same company or at another company. You might have to fire your boss and find another opportunity.

Keep Boundaries about your goals
Having healthy boundaries is critical to your success. Without healthy boundaries you can attract people into your life that do not mean well for you. Boundaries are things that we often have as children, but then as adults we forget the importance of implementing them. An example of a boundary that our parents give us is a bedtime. Children respond better when there are strict

boundaries in place and adults do as well. When boundaries are in place life runs smoother. The fact of the matter is that without boundaries you will be negatively impacted. Boundaries set the tone for our expectations and are a sign of self-respect. We all deserve healthy boundaries. It is crucial to our success. There will always be someone who wants to challenge your boundaries. The steps below will give you practical steps to apply when this happens and skills to stand firm when implementing boundaries.

1. It is important to first consider your past. Think about what has worked for you and what has not. Identify boundaries that you can put in place to prevent the pitfalls from happening. For example has it worked for you to have your phone on when you are in the middle of typing a paper? Or has it worked for you to have friends over while you are prepping for a work presentation? My guess is that it has not. Now that you are aware of those things, set boundaries around making those situations work for you. An example boundary may be that while I am typing papers I will turn my phone off that way I am not tempted to answer calls or check notifications.
2. Identify the boundaries for each area of your life. The reason you will want to separate each individual area is because each one will have different boundaries. For example a work boundary may be that you do not complete any work related tasks on the weekend. This same boundary cannot apply to your family, as you may be a parent and we all know that job does not stop on the weekend.
3. Give yourself permission to accept and follow the boundaries you have listed. Fear and guilt are the two emotions people often feel when setting up boundaries. In order to challenge that guilt and fear list all of the ways benefits of setting these boundaries. The benefits of setting boundaries are endless. Some examples include; increased productivity, more time for things that matter, boundaries set the tone for your expectations and lastly they protect you. It is important to know that the person who is angry with you for setting a boundary is the person with the problem. Not the other way around.

4. Make self-care a priority. When you practice self-care you are putting yourself first. The truth is that you aren't good to anyone unless you are first good to yourself. The more you care for yourself the more you are able to recognize the importance of boundaries.
5. Take it one step at a time and start small. When building boundaries it is important that you do not overwhelm yourself. Prior to your beginning of building boundaries you were used to not having them. Therefore, if you just dived in it may feel overwhelming or it may not feel quite "right" to you. Start with a small boundary that is not threatening to you and then build from there.

1. What situations have caused major interruptions in my day due to a lack of boundaries?
    1.
    2.
    3.

2. How can I change each one to allow myself to be more productive?
    1.
    2.
    3.

3. What boundaries or actions are acceptable for each area of my life?

Work_____

Friendships_____

Family_____

Acquantainces_____

Strangers_____

Other_____

4. What ways can I prevent the guilt that I feel when setting boundaries?

5. What are the consequences of not setting up boundaries?

6. What self-care activities have I practice today?

7. What self-care activities will I make a priority to practice this week?

Getting rid of your distractions
Distractions can also be contributors to clutter by diverting your attention from what's important and allowing clutter to grow. Procrastination is a self-created phenomenon that everyone faces. You never feel good while procrastinating. The work that you're avoiding is still hanging over your head. No distraction is enough to completely eliminate that nagging feeling. You continue to check the time and shift your attention back and forth between the distraction and the work you should be doing. The result is mental clutter. Some distractions aren't all that distracting. They just happen to be a more enjoyable option than the work you should be doing. However, some distractions are highly distracting in their own right. Evaluate the distractions you face in your life each day:

1. How do you waste time? Forget about procrastinating. If you have nothing pressing on your schedule, how do you waste time? Make a list. A few common ways in which we waste our time:

- Social media
- Spending time with friends when we should be working

- Doing meaningless tasks just for the sake of saying that we are working.

Ask yourself why haven't you already reached this goal? Allow yourself to give no excuses. The reasons that I see to be common is lack of productivity, lack of discipline, lack of direction and confusion about a skill needed. These are all things that can be learned. They should never be obstacles to your success.

It is important for us to recognize things that are killing our productivity. When it comes to time management we can be our own worst enemy. Here is how you can cut down on some of the biggest distractions:

1. Social media. Social media has its pros and cons. How many of you say you will get on social media really quick and before you know it you are on your best friend's old roommate's ex-boyfriends page? Social media can be a major time sucker. To prevent yourself from getting consumed in the world of social media schedule social media time. So when you are making a plan for the week ahead maybe set out 15 a day that you will use on social media. You really do not need much time on social media unless you have a business you're trying to promote. Also make a plan for what you are doing so you can make sure you are on task. If you want to log on to a support group make sure you do just that. If you want to log on and watch a friend's live post, make sure you're doing that. If your goal is to check in with your uncle out of town by checking his page, stick to it. Set a timer for the amount of time. That way when the timer goes off you know it is time for you to get off.

2. Television. This can be a great source of entertainment during your downtime. I even sometimes will watch Law and Order as a downtime activity. I refer to this as a "me time" activity. When the show goes off, I get off. In total I do not watch more than two hours of TV in total per week. I can tell you first hand that this decision to cut down on my TV time has been one of the biggest contributors to my success. The truth is that TV is a lot like social media. You start watching it and before you know it you have lost three hours of your time. To reduce the amount of TV time, make a schedule for it as

well and if you find it necessary, set an alarm so you do not suck up your time on things that are not pushing you closer to your goals.

3. Friends and family. Our friends and family are great people but sometimes they do not understand everything we have planned out to accomplish our goals. Therefore they may reach out because they want you to go out with them Saturday or because they want to have a dinner date. It's not up to your friend or family member to know your plans. This is exactly why you need to be clear about when you are and are not available. It is your job to respect your time. In order to do that you must be secure enough to tell your friends what days and times will not work for you. Do not alter your plans to fit someone else's schedule because you're the only who will lose out. I plan my week ahead and put down every task, including me time, if I have a task scheduled and someone asks me to do something I politely decline and immediately try to schedule out when it can happen. This gives me a chance to still do what I set out to do, but it also does not make my friend or family member feel as though I am neglecting them.

4. Being overwhelmed. The truth is when you get in the state of feeling overwhelmed it actually does throw you off task. When you get to the point of your to do list being so big that you don't know where to begin, many people just shut down instead. You feel hopeless and stuck and oftentimes you just stop. To combat the feeling of being overwhelmed make a to-do list and break your plans up into smaller chunks. Also be realistic about what you can accomplish in a certain amount of time. This will help you to not feel as overwhelmed. Once you start checking off your tasks you will feel more accomplished and less distracted.

Declutter your mind

Tip 1: Identify what you need to be successful
To achieve big goals you will need support. You must have the right network in place in advance or you will increase the likelihood of failing. Do you need help from people? Do you need money to achieve this goal? Do you need more time? Without identifying this, you will have challenges with reaching your goals. Once you

identify this you can move to step ask yourself how you can acquire the resources you need to be successful? Will you need to ask your spouse to take on a bigger responsibility at home? If you do this you will increase the likelihood of success. You will also see that the goal seems more feasible than when you first began.

Tip 2: Overcome limiting beliefs
You must get your mind ready to build your dreams! Do you know you are your own worst enemy? What do you believe about your own success? Do you believe that you can set and reach goals? Do you believe that you can be successful? Do you believe there is a purpose behind setting your goals? If you let it, your subconscious mind will trick you. Have you ever avoided writing down a goal because then you will have to face your failure? That is your subconscious mind trying to distract you. You are actually more likely to reach your goals.

Fear, insecurity and doubt are limiting beliefs that keep you stagnant. These behaviors are not based on reality. We know that these beliefs are false, however we sometimes embrace them as truth. When our beliefs are limited, we limit our perception and experience of what is possible. The best way to overcome these limiting beliefs is to tell yourself that they are not your reality. These beliefs are not true. You have to believe that. Some common misconceptions that I hear are:

- I don't have this skill.
- I'm not good at this.
- Others can do it better than me.
- I'm not experienced enough.
- I'm not smart enough.
- I'm not important enough.
- I'm too young.
- I'm too old.
- I don't have the money.

In addition to negative misconceptions here are some limiting beliefs that could negatively impact your success when setting goals:

- Guilt
- Worry

- Regret
- Comparing yourself to others
- Gaining self-esteem through pleasing others
- Mentally checking out when faced with stressful situations
- Worrying about what others think of you
- Expecting the worst
- Thinking about the past and the future

Contemplate on whether you struggle with any of these negative mental habits. Yes, it is great to know what can impact you, but the real question is how to fix it. How can you set yourself up for success with all of these things standing in the way? The best way is to quickly deal with your negative thoughts. Listed below is how you can get in control of the negative thoughts:

1. Understand that your negative thoughts are hurting you. 99% of your worries and negative self-talk are harming you. Believe that simple fact and you're halfway to freedom.
2. Be observant. Notice when you're having a negative thought.
3. Replace the thought. Reverse the thought. Tell yourself that you're good enough. Tell yourself that things will be okay. Is it true? Well, it's no more of a lie than telling yourself something negative. At least you'll feel better and be in a better position to thrive. Considering that things usually work out, it's more accurate than your negative thoughts

Tip 3: Discipline yourself
Identify what you need to accomplish. Start on the most important task first. Do not move on until this task is done. This will get the most difficult task out the way and actually make you feel accomplished to work on your other goals. Another way to discipline yourself is to remove all distractions. This may mean turning your phone off while working or DVR your favorite show so you don't feel rushed to try to catch up on it. When you remove the distractions

you are less likely to get pulled away from what it is that you are working on.

I have also found that telling people about your goals improves your discipline because now you are accountable to reaching those goals. You do not want to look like a failure or let anyone down.

Tip 4: Take care of yourself
Working on goals is difficult and can take a lot out of you but it is well worth it in the end. Here are some tips that you can use to improve your self-care and your overall success. Do not allow yourself to feel guilty by prioritizing your needs and your self-care. Without consistent self-care you won't be good to anyone else.

Listed below are 25 ways that you can take care of yourself. Try one out today, but make it a point to become consistent:

1. Say no to anything that is not important to you. Reducing the amount of unneeded responsibility reduces the burden you're feeling.
2. Do not be afraid to ask for help. People won't know you need them unless you verbalize it.
3. Make sleep a priority. Not just any sleep, but enough sleep. Work is never more important than sleep. If you can add in naps they allow you to rejuvenate yourself in the middle of the day and wake up with new motivation and momentum to keep pushing through the day.
4. Take mini breaks throughout the day. The change in routine will make it easier to begin your task again.
5. Keep in touch with people who care about you. Isolation is dangerous.
6. Write down five things you are grateful every morning. Doing this will help you to shift into a more optimistic focus.
7. Highlight your accomplishments. This allows you to remember what you have accomplished when you feel hopeless.
8. Reduce media usage. Don't overflow your brain with the news or social media. This can cause distractions.
9. Write down affirmations and put them in a jar. This is my favorite. When feeling sad, overwhelmed or defeated grab one. This helps you remember your strengths and changes your focus.

10. Smile. Forcing yourself to smile can boost your mood.
11. Do something silly. We all deserve a little fun. It helps to boost and even soften your mood.
12. Single tasking. Although we become accustomed to multitasking, the truth is single tasking can actually be more productive because time is not being split between multiple projects.
13. Clear up clutter. Clutter can be distracting. Removing it can increase productivity and reduce the feeling of being overwhelmed. I spent four days de-cluttering my entire house and it was amazing.
14. Light candles. Candles allow us to relax. Who can't use a little more relaxation?
15. Take a yoga class. This helps to recharge your mind, body and soul.
16. Eat a healthy meal and drink water. Good nutrition is important to having a healthy lifestyle. This helps to nourish and hydrate your body.
17. Meditate daily for at least five minutes. Stillness really makes a huge difference. This helps you to recharge.
18. Take a walk. Walking produces endorphins and helps us to feel better.
19. Exercise regularly. This helps to increase your energy.
20. Take one day off a week. This allows you to recharge and prevents burnout. After all, that is what God did with the Sabbath and we are no better or stronger than God. We must follow His example.
21. Change your environment. Post up motivational quotes or inspiring photos. When having a rough day this can help you shift your focus and become more appreciative.
22. Compliment yourself. This positive talk will help you to feel more content and happy. It can also help to reduce the desire to be perfect.
23. Take a bath. This can help relax you and help you to fall asleep.
24. Reward yourself. This helps to increase your motivation and encourages you to stay on the right path. It does not always have to be financial either. You can reward yourself with extra TV time or that lunch date with a friend you have been putting off.
25. Deep breathing. This helps to reduce tension and relaxes the mind and body.

Here is a check list that you can use to ensure that you are taking care of yourself in every area of your life:

Physical Self-Care
___ Eat regularly (e.g. breakfast, lunch and dinner)
___ Eat healthy
___ Exercise
___ Get regular medical care for prevention
___ Get medical care when needed
___ Take time off when needed
___ Get massages
___ Dance, swim, walk, run, play sports, sing, or do some other physical activity that is fun
___ Get enough sleep
___ Wear clothes you like
___ Take vacations
___ Take day trips or mini-vacations
___ Make time away from telephones
___ Other:

Psychological Self-Care
___ Make time for self-reflection
___ Have your own personal psychotherapy
___ Write in a journal
___ Read literature that is unrelated to work
___ Do something at which you are not expert or in charge of
___ Decrease stress in your life
___ Share different aspects of yourself with others
___ Notice your inner experience
___ Listen to your thoughts, judgments, beliefs, attitudes, and feelings
___ Engage your intelligence in a new area, e.g. go to an art museum, history exhibit, sports event, auction, theater performance
___ Practice receiving from others
___ Be curious
___ Say "no" to extra responsibilities sometimes
___ Other:

Emotional Self-Care
___ Spend time with others whose company you enjoy
___ Stay in contact with important people in your life
___ Give yourself affirmations, praise yourself
___ Love yourself
___ Re-read favorite books, review favorite movies
___ Identify comforting activities, objects, people, relationships, places and seek them out
___ Allow yourself to cry
___ Find things that make you laugh
___ Express your outrage in social action, letters and donations, marches, protests
___ Play with children
___ Other:

Spiritual Self-Care
___ Make time for reflection
___ Spend time with nature
___ Find a spiritual connection or community
___ Be open to inspiration
___ Cherish your optimism and hope
___ Be aware of nonmaterial aspects of life
___ Identify what in meaningful to you and notice its place in your life
___ Meditate
___ Pray
___ Sing
___ Spend time with children
___ Have experiences of awe
___ Contribute to causes in which you believe
___ Read inspirational literature (talks, music, etc.)
___ Other:

Workplace, Entrepreneurial or Professional Self-Care
___ Take a break during the workday (e.g. lunch)
___ Take time to chat with co-workers
___ Make quiet time to complete tasks
___ Identify projects or tasks that are exciting and rewarding
___ Set limits with your clients and colleagues

___ Balance your caseload so that no one day or part of a day is "too much"
___ Arrange your work space so it is comfortable and comforting
___ Get regular supervision or consultation
___ Negotiate for your needs (benefits, pay raise)
___ Have a peer support group
___ Develop a non-trauma area of professional interest
___ Other:

Balance
___ Strive for balance within your work-life and workday
___ Strive for balance among work, family, relationships, play and rest

Tip 5: Avoid the temptation to quit

There are many times and many different reasons that we want to give up. There's an old Chinese proverb that says: "The temptation to quit will be greatest just before you are about to succeed." I found this to be true for each of my business startups. How many times have we given up just to look back with frustration that we gave up too quickly? The temptation to quit will always be there, but we do not have to feed into that temptation. Listed below are five things we can do to avoid giving up.

1. Find an accountability partner. It is important that we identify someone we are close with who will help to push us. Accountability partners require you to take responsibility and also helps you to stay true to your commitment. Make sure to maintain constant communication with your accountability partner.

2. Be sure to single task. Sometimes we want to quit because we are overwhelmed and the tasks seem unbearable. Single tasking takes the pressure off and contributes to higher productivity. This, in turn, is motivating.

3. Sleep on the decision. As women, we often react emotionally. Instead of being brash in decision making, it is imperative to think through decisions and all of the potential outcomes. If you give yourself a day it allows you to be sure that you are making the right decision.

4. Identify why you began. If you spend fifteen minutes writing down what you were working for, it may trigger you to remember why you started. It is also helpful to make note of accomplishments. The point of doing this is to make it clear that going forward is the only viable option.

5. Review your expectations. Expectations change your perception of reality and can cause you to feel discouraged. Rome was not built in a day. We have to remember this is the same for our goals in life as well. If you realize your expectations are unattainable, try to redefine them. The goal should be to create growth, but not at the cost of you causing yourself to feel overwhelmed.

Maintain your goals

"Obstacles are the frightful things you see when you take your eyes off your goals."
- Henry Ford

Starting to work towards a goal is one thing. Maintaining the momentum is something completely different. Many times we set goals and fall off just a few short days later. Maybe you said you would eat healthy, but then your job buys donuts for the staff. Now healthy eating has been thrown on the back burner. That happens to the best of us. As a matter of fact, the example I just gave actually happened to me. I am here to share with you that it does not have to be that way forever. I want to share how you can maintain your motivation no matter what temptations come your way or no matter how appealing quitting seems.

Imagine how much more you could accomplish if you could stick to your goals. How many times have you resolved to go on a diet or look for a more rewarding job, only to find yourself back to your old habits within a few days? While you may be motivated to make positive changes in your life, it's also important to use strategies that will make you more productive. It is great to set a goal and even better to work at it diligently. The trouble comes when you lose the momentum and you start to fall off. I have some key steps to share that will encourage you maintain working on your goals.

The first step is to **announce your intentions.** Letting others know what you have in mind increases the pressure in a good way. You'll feel more accountable about living up to your claims. The second step is to **ask for help.** You can accomplish more when you're willing to accept support and feedback. Team up with a friend or colleague with similar interests. Thank your family for believing in you. The third step is to **automate your choices.** Turn smart decisions into habits. If you speak up in meetings on a regular basis, you'll feel less anxious about saying what's on your mind. Automating your choices will eliminate the nonessentials in order to make time in your schedule for the things that are important. Sometimes we make commitments that seem important at first, but then we realize that they're not. These things might actually be counterproductive to what we want to accomplish. When that happens it is okay to change what is on your calendar.

One of the most important steps is to **minimize distractions.** Turn off the TV and limit your online browsing. Free up your leisure hours for more meaningful activities. The fifth step is to **develop a growth mindset.** Remember that your intelligence and talents are not fixed quantities beyond your control. You can grow smarter and more accomplished when you apply yourself in any area where you want to stretch your skills. The sixth step is to be sure to **manage your stress.** The truth is that stress can sabotage your dreams. Be sure to nourish your body and mind with nutritious food, regular exercise, and adequate rest so you're ready to take on new demands. An important thing to do is to **reward yourself.** A lot of people often overlook this aspect. Be sure to take good care of yourself when working on your goals. Give yourself incentives along the way. Treat yourself to your favorite coffee drink or a lunch date with a good friend. The last step is to **hang in there.** Perseverance pays off and I know this first hand. Think long term and make plans for how to deal with obstacles so you can pick yourself back up when you slip. We all slip when stepping into uncharted territory, and that is okay. Just be sure you have developed a plan to address it accordingly. If you want to enjoy more success, set concrete goals and write them down. Strengthening your goals will help keep you motivated and increase your chances of reaching your objectives.

Quitting Your Goals

"Sometimes you have to know when enough is good enough."
-Nicolya

It only takes a few seconds on social media to find quotes that remind you that "champions don't quit" or that "quitting lasts forever. Such "inspirational" quotes and "motivational" images send the message that if you give up on a goal you've given up on *life*. One quote that comes to my mind is "If it's a priority you won't stop working towards it". In reality, it is instilled in us that we are not allowed to quit. How many times have you been told to finish your plate as a child?

Whether you've set your sights on running a 10K, or turning your part-time hobby into a full-time business, the path to achievement doesn't always come in a straight line. While there's a lot to be said for perseverance, sometimes it does make more sense to walk away. What you need to remember is that quitting doesn't mean you're a loser. In fact, it often takes incredible strength and faith to step away from a goal you've set for yourself. But how do you know when to give up without feeling like a quitter?

Here are five signs that it is okay to give yourself permission to quit working on a goal:

1. Your goals have changed. I discussed this earlier. Our lives change daily and therefore it is highly likely that your goals will change too. Many people feel like once they've set a goal for themselves that they have to keep going especially if they've told other people about it. I was guilty of that. I felt like if I started something I had to finish it even if it no longer aligned with what I wanted. Do you know how many books I wasted my time reading even though I hated them from the beginning? I kept going anyways just to say I did. I stayed at jobs that no longer matched my desire or career path all because I hate quitting. The truth is just because you set a goal for yourself, that doesn't mean that you have to commit yourself to accomplishing it. Often, a goal that seemed like a good idea six months ago is no longer important and you need to adjust to this new reality. As you grow and change, you'll likely outgrow some old goals, and the best (and often only) way to make room for new ones is to abandon some of your current plans.

2. The process doesn't align with your values. While a goal may sound honorable in the beginning, you may discover that the process of getting there might not align with your values. I remember I worked at a call center in college and part of my salary was to sell common carrier insurance (insurance for airplanes) to the elderly. The truth is the people I was selling to did not ride airplanes. The company was a scam. Although the money was great and I needed it to pay off a credit card, it went against my belief of treating people how I would want to be treated. I would never be okay with someone taking advantage of my grandmother and I needed to treat those clients with the same respect. Living according to your values is key to a successful life. Don't abandon yours in an effort just to prove to yourself—or anyone else—that you can reach a goal.

3. The reward isn't worth it. Sometimes we set a goal but the outcome or reward is not truly valuable. Ask yourself: Is the reward truly worth the effort I'm putting in? There's no shame in admitting that the goal just may not be worth the time or energy it's going to take to get there.

4. You've dug yourself into a hole. Whether you've invested a lot of money in a business that just isn't working, or you've devoted endless hours to a project that no longer seems viable, knowing that you've dug yourself into a hole can be really frustrating. But despite the gloomy outlook, it can be tempting to keep going. When you step back and look at things objectively, the idea of "I've invested this much, I might as well keep going," doesn't always make sense. Do not commit to a mistake just because of the time you spent investing into it. I dealt with that in my skin care business. I started selling skin care in the beginning and was making money. After a while I started losing money with the business and my focus was elsewhere. I kept going just to ensure I was not giving up but there was a huge hole I was digging each month. It was a big pill to swallow, but once I did the outcome was much prettier than I assumed it would be. I was not spending money on the mandated products each month, I was no longer throwing parties that no one attended and I freed up my time to focus on my coaching business.

5. The risks outweigh the benefit. Sometimes, excitement over the potential benefits of reaching a goal can cloud your judgment and cause you to overlook the risks it will take to get there. If pursuing a goal has a negative impact on your health, relationships, or finances, rethink your options. My ex-husband took a job out of the city and lived away Monday- Friday. I thought the benefits would be great but it put a major strain on our already toxic relationship. In this situation the risks were too big and I should have thought of those instead of focusing on the benefits. Sometimes, the risk is just too great. Give yourself the time to carefully calculate the risk associated with reaching your goal. Monitor the cost and be willing to step away when the risk outweighs the potential reward.

So now that you know that quitting is okay in certain situations how do you go about it? Quitting a goal shouldn't be a decision you take lightly or do with haste. Just because you feel tired, frustrated, or disappointed today doesn't mean you should give up. Make your decision based on a careful balance between emotion and logic. Take time to really think about the pros and cons of continuing vs. the pros and the cons of quitting. And remember: Choosing to walk away *doesn't* mean you're a failure. Giving up on today's goal could actually be a stepping stone to greater future success.

Conclusion

"You have to set goals that are almost out of reach. If you set a goal that is attainable without much work or thought, you are stuck with something below your true talent and potential."
- Steve Garvey

So we have learned how to overcome our fears, to conquer our mindset and to create a plan. Now what do you do when you are running out of strength to keep going?

The truth is this happens to the best of us. I call myself the goal setting guru, but even I get tired of working on my goals. Even I run into delays that make me wish I never started. Even I have days where I set aside time to work and I have not one ounce of motivation to do it. Even I get distracted by my phone, social media or things going on in my life. To be quite honest, I have published four other books, over fifty e-books and when I set out to write this book I ran into every delay imaginable. Each delay was one more thing that made me want to give up. First my dear associate Nik Carson who wrote the foreword was a victim of Hurricane Irma so the deadlines had to be pushed back by several weeks. My divorce process had gotten worse and I had absolutely no motivation to write. Lastly, the health of my grandmother declined so rapidly that we started to look at homes for her to stay in and prepared for the likelihood of losing her soon. I can certainly relate to your exhaustion, frustration, distractions and confusion. I need to share with you the strategies that I use to keep going when the process gets tough.

Whatever you do, DON'T STOP. When you feel like quitting follow these quick tips to rejuvenate yourself!

1. Remember why you started! Pull pen and paper out and write down three reasons that you set this goal to begin with. Is it because you wanted more time freedom to be able to do after school stuff with your kiddos? Is it because you wanted to be healthier? Is it because you want to help other people? To take your family on that big vacation you've been talking about? Have an extra stream of income? Pay down debt? It always helps to go back to the beginning and remember why this goal was so important. If the goal is not important you will not believe in it and you will never make it a priority.

2. Look back to where you started. Sometimes it's hard to gauge how far we have come because we spend time comparing ourselves to others or where we think we should be. The truth is that we should focus on just HOW FAR WE HAVE COME. I'd be willing to bet it's

a lot further than you realize. This is why I often journal my progress because it serves as a quick reminder of the steps I have made thus far.

3. Think of the "what ifs". What if you don't try it and what if you don't ever go for that goal that you truly desire? Don't settle for the fear, settle for the possibilities. If I had never written this book I would not have the chance to help women all around the world reach their goals. So take some time to think about what will be different if you don't go after your goal

4. Change your environment. Your current environment reflects your current life, goals and thoughts. Now is the time to change the environment to reflect what you desire soon. When working on my goals, I often change my environment to reflect what it is that I desire. For example this year I set a goal to complete the mindful 20/30 challenge. If you're not familiar with this challenge I will explain it. The mindful 20/30 challenge is meditating for twenty minutes every day for thirty days straight. For this goal I went and got decorative pillows and I pulled out an old journal to write down my thoughts. I beautified the space where I would be meditating in order to make the goal process more inviting. The practice of changing my environment really helps me to align my day-to-day actions with the goal I desire to accomplish. Take a minute to ask yourself: What do you have in your environment that is in alignment with your goals or what do you have around you that reminds you to work diligently towards them each day? In addition to decorative objects I often hang up motivational quotes because just like everyone else I often want to give up. These quotes inspire me in some of my most difficult moments. Since they have helped me I thought it would be helpful to share some quotes related to goal setting that have helped me in my process.

What you get by achieving your goals is not as important as what you become by achieving your goals." -Zig Ziglar

Then the LORD answered me and said, "Write the vision
and engrave it plainly on [clay] tablets so that the one who reads it

will run. "For the vision is yet for the appointed [future] time
It hurries toward the goal [of fulfillment]; it will not fail.
Even though it delays, wait [patiently] for it,
Because it will certainly come; it will not delay.
-Habakkuk 2:2-3 (AMP)

If you go to work on your goals, your goals will go to work on you.
If you go to work on your plan, your plan will go to work on you.
Whatever good things we build end up building us. - Jim Rohn

    Please feel free to steal some of these quotes or add some of your own and hang them in a place where you can see them often. It will serve as a reminder that working toward your goals is beyond worth it.
    Setting and reaching goals takes time. It is not something that happens overnight! We must let go of the microwave mentality. Take the information you read and make a plan for your next steps. When you go to sleep with a plan you will wake up with a purpose! Become overcommitted to reaching your goals; that's where your success will start. If you walk away from this book without implementing what you have learned do not be surprised if you don't live the life you want! Now is not the time to doubt yourself or review all of your fears. Now is the time to take what you learned and push harder than you could ever imagine!!
    You must remember that there is no end to goal setting. Once you reach the goal you set you should then aim to work on another goal. In reality we are designed to be working toward our goals on a regular basis. Think about it, aren't you happy when you are striving toward your potential? If so don't stop there. Continue to apply these steps to the goals you desire now and in the future. Zig Ziglar said it best: "A goal properly set is halfway reached". You are halfway there lady, keep it going!
    Finally I have a goal setting reflection piece that I would like to share with you. Someone shared it with me when I began my coaching business and I feel inspired to share it with others. Please feel free to use it as you're working on your goals.

My goals motivate me.

Goals give me something to strive for. My goals make me excited about making positive changes in my life. I make concrete plans. I decide what I need to do and when I need to do it.

I start small and I'm high. I take baby steps at first.

Each victory builds my confidence. I know that I can tackle bigger things. My ambitions continue to grow. I prove to myself that I am capable and strong.

I gather feedback and support. I ask others for their comments and advice. I phone a friend when I need a pep talk to keep pushing.

I strengthen my commitment to my goals daily. I think about how my goals will align with my values. I even use visualization practice is to increase my dedication to my goals.

I remain flexible. When time passes by I come up with alternative plans to make sure I fill in the time to work towards my goals.

My goals give me a sense of direction. I know where I am heading and the milestones that I need to reach along the way.

I take charge of my life instead of drifting along or reacting to outside events.

My goals encourage me to be persistent. I enjoy each stage of the journey. I keep going even when I encounter obstacles. Michael's encourage me to be persistent. I enjoy each age of the journey. I keep going even when I encounter obstacles.

My goals challenge me to be creative. I work smarter so I can beat my own record. I create conditions to help me succeed.

Today I keep my purpose in mind. I love the satisfaction that comes when I reach each of my goals!

Reflection

What is my biggest take away from *The Goal Getter Guide*?

What advancements have I made thus far as it relates to my goal?

What actions and thoughts will I change to be more effective at working toward my goals?

I have included a reflection journal in Appendix A. Take time to review where you started and where you are now. I have also included three goal setting guide templates in Appendix B. Use these as guides to write out your three most pressing goals.

Appendix A: Reflection Journal

Former accomplishments

What are the biggest accomplishments I have made in life?

Why does this make me proud?

What steps did I take to reach this part of my life?

What things did I avoid?

Who did I have in my corner?

Last year's reflection

What steps did I take last year that I am proud of?

What steps did I take last year got in the way of my goals?

What did I learn from last year?

What do I hope does not follow me into future years?

What opportunities did I miss this year?

What reason did I miss these chances?

This year's desires

What do I want more of this year?

What will I do different this year?

Why is this important?

What emotions will impact me both positively and negatively?

What can I do to foster the poster and ignore the negative?

Future plans

Where do I see myself in five years?

What vision to you have for yourself and your family?

How will your steps today increase your future goals?

Appendix B: Goal Setting Guide

Goal Setting Guide

What is my goal?
_____
_____

It is important for me to achieve this goal because:
_____
_____

Steps I need to take to achieve this goal:
_____
_____

The skills and knowledge I need to be successful:
_____
_____

Who can help me?
_____
_____

What motivates me to reach this goal?
_____
_____

How will I know when I have reached this goal?
_____
_____

Have you ensured that your goal follows the golden goal-setting rule?

G
O
A
L

Notes:

Goal Setting Guide

What is my goal?
_____
_____

It is important for me to achieve this goal because:
_____
_____

Steps I need to take to achieve this goal:
_____
_____

The skills and knowledge I need to be successful:
_____
_____

Who can help me?
_____
_____

What motivates me to reach this goal?
_____
_____

How will I know when I have reached this goal?
_____
_____

Have you ensured that your goal follows the golden goal-setting rule?

G
O
A
L

Notes:

Goal Setting Guide

What is my goal?
_____
_____

It is important for me to achieve this goal because:
_____
_____

Steps I need to take to achieve this goal:
_____
_____

The skills and knowledge I need to be successful:
_____
_____

Who can help me?
_____
_____

What motivates me to reach this goal?
_____
_____

How will I know when I have reached this goal?
_____
_____

Have you ensured that your goal follows the golden goal-setting rule?

G
O
A
L

Notes:

About Nicolya

Nicolya Williams is the type of woman who pursues her goals with passion and determination. She is dedicated to helping other women conquer their chaos and reach their goals. Nicolya is a personal development coach, radio host, best-selling author, and blogger for women. Nicolya graduated from The Ohio State University (B.A., Psychology) and obtained her M.Ed. from the University of Dayton with a focus on Clinical Counseling and School Counseling. She is currently a doctoral student with a focus on Transformational Leadership. Nicolya holds a Coach Practitioner certificate and is licensed as both a Community Counselor and School Counselor, with a Chemical Dependency Counselor Assistant license.

Nicolya is a lifelong learner who strives to continue her personal growth through reading and interacting with her social and spiritual community. She is an avid reader and is devoted to building up her own strong women; her daughters, Kaelyn and Kamryn. Nicolya is committed to creating a space for women to be heard and successful! You can connect with Nicolya at www.nicolyawilliams.com or on all social media platforms via @NicolyaWilliams. You can also check out Nicolya's other books on Amazon!

About Nik Carson

After leaving the medical field of 24 years, Nichole "Nik" Carson made the decision to step out on faith and out of her comfort zone and start living the life that God has purposed by not settling for less and removing the limits from her life and from God.
Her platform to Living a Limitless Lifestyle and how to view success and failure from a Godly perspective is her mission. This is what she lives and coaches.

Nichole 'Nik" Carson is a Powerful and Influential Author, Speaker, Lifestyle Coach, Entrepreneur and Mother. Her testimony and her message will help give you the inspiration and motivation needed to point you into the right direction on your journey. Because the only limits in life are the ones that we create.

Social Media:
www.facebook.com/nikcarson1
www.instagram.com/nikcarson1
Website:
www.nikcarson.com

Clarity Cove Publishing
~We publish books the world needs~

Clarity Cove Publishing was created by Nicolya Williams. Clarity Cove Publishing connects with powerful, determined and driven women to help them turn their message into their masterpiece. We offer publishing services, writing assistance, marketing strategies and much more. Our vision is to foster creativity, encourage risk taking and increase clarity around your book writing goals. Our authors have an opportunity to get their message out into the masses without losing their authenticity in the process.

To inquire about publishing with us or getting support along your publishing journey reach out to us at
http://www.nicolyawilliams.com/clarity-cove-publishing/
or email at claritycove@nicolyawilliams.com

www.ingramcontent.com/pod-product-compliance
Lightning Source LLC
Chambersburg PA
CBHW071726040426
42446CB00011B/2238